Carl Jung
The Godfather of Shadow Work

by
Jason A. Solomon, B.Ed.

© 2025 Jason A Solomon, B.Ed
All rights reserved.
No part of this publication may be reproduced, distributed, or transmitted in any form or by any means, including photocopying, recording, or other electronic or mechanical methods, without the prior written permission of the author, except in the case of brief quotations embodied in critical reviews and certain other non-commercial uses permitted by copyright law.

For permission requests, contact the publisher or author through official channels.

Title: Carl Jung The Godfather of Shadow Work
Author: Jason A Solomon, B.Ed
First Edition: 2025
ISBN: 978-1-7642115-2-9
Cover design and interior layout by Aussie Guy's Books
"THE GODFATHER Version 2" font was created by Jeff Bell for www.geocities.com/boltonbroscom
This is a work of nonfiction. Names and identifying details may have been changed to protect individuals and their privacy.

DEDICATION

TO THOSE WHO HAVE DARED TO LOOK INWARD,

AND TO THOSE WHO ARE STILL AFRAID OF WHAT THEY MIGHT FIND.

THIS BOOK IS FOR YOU.

Epigraph

"Until you make the unconscious conscious, it will direct your life and you will call it fate."

- Carl Gustav Jung

Preface

There are moments in life when the mirror I look into is not glass but shadow. I discovered this during my own journey of silence, stillness, and confronting the darker layers of myself. In those moments I began to understand why Carl Gustav Jung was not just another thinker, but the Godfather of Shadow Work, the one who dared to name what most of us run from, the unseen forces of the unconscious.

This book is part of my Shadow Work Psychology series, which includes Shadow Work Demystified, Shadow Work Evolution, and Activate the Subconscious. Each of these works stands on its own, yet together they form a path of inner excavation. Where Shadow Work Demystified lays out the fundamentals, Shadow Work Evolution deepens the practice, and Activate the Subconscious guides us into alignment, this volume honours the original source, Jung himself, and asks what it means to confront the shadow with reverence, curiosity, and courage.

This is not a textbook of Jungian psychology. It is a bridge between Jung's insights and the lived experience of shadow work today.

Jung wrote of the Self, the archetypes, and the collective unconscious, but his greatest legacy may be the invitation to meet ourselves honestly, in light and in darkness.

If you have read the earlier works in this series, you will find echoes here, reminders, threads, and continuations of the journey we have already walked together. If this is your first step into shadow work, know that you are entering through the doorway of its true architect.

I am not writing this book to glorify Jung as a man. Like all of us, he was flawed, human, and often conflicted. But as a guide, as the one who gave us the language of the shadow, he remains a figure whose ideas continue to provoke, heal, and transform.

My hope is that this book serves as both a tribute and a challenge, a tribute to Jung's courage, and a challenge to each of us to begin or to continue our own shadow work with honesty and humility.

~ Jason A. Solomon, B.Ed.

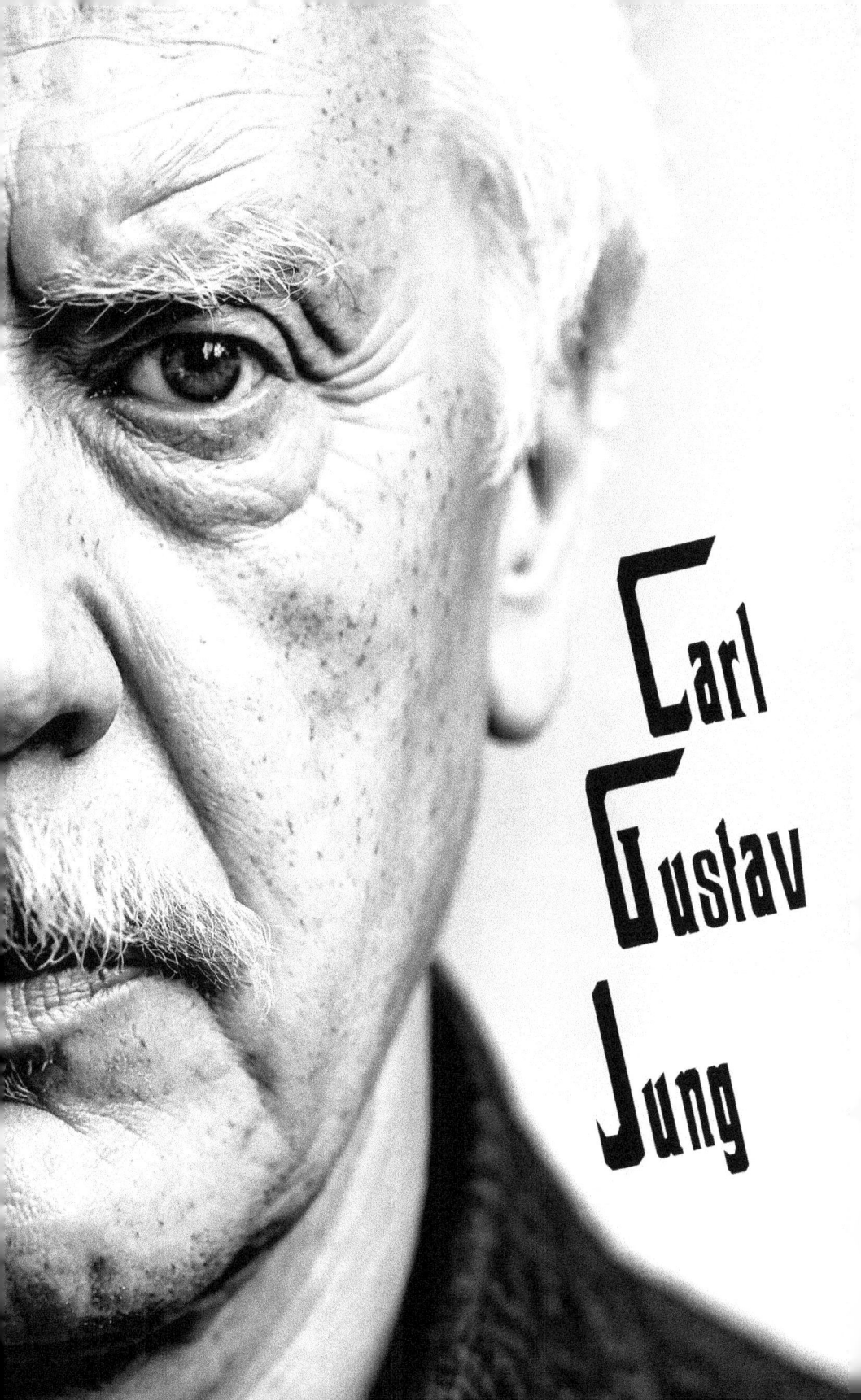

TABLE OF CONTENTS

Preface 9

Why Jung Still Matters...15

Carl Jung and the Birth of Shadow Work 19

    The Godfather of the Unconscious 21

    The Psyche & Its Architecture......................................27

    Persona, Shadow, & the Masks We Wear 32

The Growing Practice of Shadow Work 37

    Naming the Darkness...39

    Dreams That Speak..43

    Archetypes Alive Within 48

    Battle Between Light & Dark 53

    The Steps of Integration 58

    Active Imagination & Dialogue with the Shadow.................61

Individuation and the Self..65

    Individuation & Becoming Whole................................67

    Fear, Failure, & the Tasks That Shape Us....................71

    Light & Dark Together – Living Beyond Illusion................75

Carl Jung in the Modern World 79

    Therapy, Self-Practice, & the Risk of Misuse 81

    The Cultural Shadow – Myths, Movies, & Archetypes.......84

    The Offer You Cannot Refuse 87

From the Author's Chair 89
Appendix 95
    Curiosity Corner 97
    References & Further Reading 101
    Companion Reading 102
    Glossary Jungian Terms 103
    In Closing 105

Introduction

Why Jung Still Matters

When I first encountered the writings of Carl Gustav Jung, I did not fully grasp their weight. At that time I was too busy chasing productivity, distractions, and the endless noise of a restless world. Yet Jung's words found their way through. They sat in my mind quietly, almost as if they were waiting for the right season of my life to bloom. What struck me most was not his complexity but his courage. He was unafraid to name the things we most wish to avoid. He was willing to stand before the shadow and say, here is the part of you that you deny, and here is the part of you that may hold your greatest treasure.

Jung matters today because we are more disconnected from ourselves than ever before. We live in an age of constant stimulation, where the pressure to present a polished persona has never been greater. We hide behind screens, filters, and carefully chosen words, yet within us the old truths remain. The shadow does not vanish simply because we distract ourselves. If anything, it grows stronger in the dark, shaping our lives without our consent. Jung warned us of this, and his warning has never been more relevant.

At the heart of Jung's psychology lies the idea of archetypes. These are not inventions of culture but deep, universal patterns within the human psyche. They live in what Jung called the collective unconscious, a shared reservoir of memory, myth, and meaning that belongs to us all. Archetypes are not fixed images, but currents of possibility that shape how we see the world and how we behave within it. The Persona, the Shadow, the Anima and Animus, and the Self are all expressions of these inner structures. They surface in dreams, in stories, in art, in religion, and in the symbols that keep repeating across centuries and cultures. To understand archetypes is to recognise that we are never entirely alone, for our inner life reflects a map that has been walked by every generation before us. For me, this realisation made shadow work feel less isolating and more like stepping into a conversation with something much larger than myself.

I have spent years exploring shadow work in my own life and through my writing. In Shadow Work Demystified I opened the doorway and explained the essentials. In Shadow Work Evolution I walked deeper into the process and how it changes us over time. In Activate the Subconscious I explored how we can align ourselves more closely with the quiet wisdom beneath the noise. This book is both a continuation and a pause. It asks me, and it asks you, to look back to where it all began, to the man who gave us the language of shadow work, and to consider what his vision still has to teach us.

Some will argue that Jung's theories are too dated for modern life, that psychology has moved on, that the self-help world has turned his ideas into something he never intended. Yet when I read his words, when I revisit his essays, lectures, and reflections, I do not hear something old. I hear something timeless. He reminds us that the task of being human has never really changed. To be human is to wrestle with what we know and what we cannot face, with the light we long to show and the darkness we hide away.

Why does Jung still matter?

Every day we see the consequences of ignoring the shadow. It spills into relationships, into politics, into culture, into every space where people gather. We project our unwanted parts onto others, condemning them for qualities we cannot admit to in ourselves. We destroy what we fear rather than asking what it might be here to teach us. Jung's work gives us a way back. It gives us the courage to turn and face what is within, and in doing so, to step closer to becoming whole.

This book is an invitation, not to worship Jung, but to walk with him. It is an attempt to honour his insights, to test them against my own lived experience, and to share with you a path that has reshaped my life. If you are willing, I ask you to read slowly, to pause when something unsettles you, and to consider what your own shadow may be trying to reveal. For me, Jung still matters because he dared to say that the darkness within us is not a curse but a calling. And I believe that if we listen, it may just change everything.

CARL JUNG AND THE BIRTH OF SHADOW WORK

Chapter 1

The Godfather of the Unconscious

A Man at the Threshold

Picture a man sitting in silence, a notebook open before him, the fire flickering in the late hours of the night. The house is quiet, the world asleep, but his mind is alive with images that feel more real than the waking day. Carl Gustav Jung was such a man. He was not a distant observer of the mind, not a detached scholar peering at patients through glass. He was a man who entered the unknown himself and returned with something to tell us.

Jung lived in the tension between two worlds. One was the polished, rational face of society, the world of science and respectability, of lectures and theories, of being seen as a professional equal to Freud. The other was the dark, irrational world of the psyche, where dreams spoke louder than words, where images carried more truth than logic, and where the soul demanded to be heard. Most of us prefer the first world. Jung risked everything to step into the second.

He returned with something radical, the recognition that the parts of ourselves we avoid are the very parts that could make us whole. He called this hidden realm the shadow, and it has haunted psychology ever since.

Jung's Descent

To understand Jung is to understand that he did not create his theories from a safe distance. He endured his own descent. When he broke from Freud, he did not simply leave behind a mentor, he walked into a wilderness. In the years that followed, Jung faced visions so intense that he feared he might be losing his sanity. Images of gods, serpents, prophets, and battles rose within him, and he chose not to run from them. Instead, he painted them, spoke to them, gave them form. This became The Red Book, a record of his confrontation with the unconscious.

Most men would have drowned in such visions. Jung allowed himself to be carried by them, trusting that even madness could hold meaning. This is why we can trust him. He did not theorise from a distance, he lived what he taught. He carried his own shadow, and rather than deny it, he entered into dialogue with it. His authority was born not from perfection but from struggle.

The Birth of the Shadow

Jung told us something we already sensed but were afraid to admit: every person carries a hidden side. The shadow is born in childhood, in those moments when we are told to stop crying, to be quiet, to be polite, to stop dreaming, to be something other than what we are. Every "do not" and every punishment teaches us which parts of ourselves are welcome and which are not. Slowly we build the Persona, the mask we wear to win love and approval, while the unwanted pieces are pushed into the dark.

This repression does not erase them. They continue to live within us, waiting, whispering, shaping our choices in ways we do not see. They rise in sudden anger, in bitter envy, in crippling insecurity.

They spill into our relationships when we lash out, when we retreat, when we sabotage what we say we want.

Jung warned us that until we make the unconscious conscious, it will rule us, and we will call it fate.

Archetypes and the Architecture of the Psyche

Jung saw more than the shadow. He recognised the very architecture of the psyche. At the surface lies the Persona, the mask of our social self. Beneath it lives the Shadow, holding all the rejected parts of us. Deeper still we encounter the Anima and Animus, the inner feminine and masculine forces that colour how we relate to ourselves and others. And at the centre lies the Self, the totality of who we are, the wholeness that calls us towards integration.

These are archetypes, universal patterns not invented by culture but inherited by every human being. They are not static images but living forces that shape our behaviour, our dreams, our myths, and our stories. The Hero, the Mother, the Wise Old Man, the Trickster, these are not simply characters of fiction, they are voices of the human soul. They appear across civilisations, across centuries, because they live within each of us.

When I first understood this, something shifted. Watching a film or reading a story was no longer entertainment alone, it was a mirror. The sacrifice of the hero reflected my own longings. The terror of the monster echoed my own fears. The betrayal, the triumph, the fall, these were not only theirs, they were mine. Jung gave us the language to see this, to know that our lives are part of a greater story, and that our inner struggles are never entirely our own.

Facing the Shadow

Jung never promised that facing the shadow would be easy. In fact, he admitted it was terrifying. "The most terrifying thing," he said, "is to accept oneself completely." Think of that for a moment. How much of yourself have you accepted, and how much do you still hide? The jealousy you deny, the anger you suppress, the desires you judge as unacceptable, these do not vanish. They wait.

And when you do not face them, they rise in disguise. You may see them in others, criticising them for flaws that secretly belong to you as well. This is projection, and it is one of the shadow's most common tricks. You call another person arrogant, while deep inside you have silenced your own longing to be seen. You judge someone for laziness, while secretly you are terrified of your own exhaustion. What you despise in others often reveals what you refuse to face in yourself.

The Teacher Within the Darkness

Here lies Jung's gift: the shadow is not only darkness. It is potential. Anger can be transformed into strength, jealousy into ambition, fear into caution, sadness into compassion. Every hidden part contains energy, and when integrated, that energy becomes a resource.

The shadow is the teacher within. To meet it is to grow. To deny it is to remain incomplete. This is why Jung insisted that individuation, the process of becoming whole, is the central task of a human life. It is not about becoming perfect, it is about becoming real.

A Personal Reflection

When I began my own shadow work, I resisted. I wanted to believe I was already strong, already in control. Yet the shadow leaked out anyway. It appeared in moments of anger I could not explain, in self-sabotage that bewildered me, in a restless dissatisfaction no achievement could quieten.

Reading Jung did not give me answers, it gave me honesty. His words were like a mirror, showing me not who I wanted to be, but who I was. At first it hurt. It felt like failure. But slowly, painfully, it became liberating. To see the shadow was to reclaim the parts of myself I had abandoned. It was to discover that even my flaws could be woven into strength.

The Godfather of Shadow Work

Why do I call Jung the Godfather of Shadow Work? Because he was the first to give us the courage to name what we deny. He was not perfect, nor was he always easy to follow. But he carried the weight of his own unconscious, and he returned to tell us that it can be survived, even transformed.

His role was not to be worshipped, but to be remembered as the one who dared to step first. He did not remove the shadow from our lives, he showed us how to face it. And in that sense, he is the Godfather, the one who held the torch at the threshold and said, "Come, there is more to you than you know."

Your Invitation

Now it is your turn. Do not read these words as theory alone. Ask yourself quietly, what is it I fear most about myself? Which memories do I avoid? Which emotions do I silence? Which traits in others disturb me because they live, unacknowledged, within me?

Take a breath. Do not rush. The shadow does not reveal itself in haste. It will wait until you are ready.

But know this: Jung's words still stand because they are true. Until you face the shadow, it will rule you. Until you accept it, you will remain divided. But once you begin, once you step into that hidden place, you may discover that the darkness you feared is not a curse at all, but the beginning of your wholeness.

Chapter 2

The Psyche & Its Architecture

When you close your eyes and allow the noise of the day to fall away, you may notice that your mind does not go silent. It begins to whisper, to drift, to form images and scenes that are sometimes clear and sometimes strange. Dreams, half-thoughts, forgotten memories, a face you have not seen for years, a fear you cannot name, all of this begins to stir. This is the psyche at work, not the surface mind that writes lists and makes decisions, but the deeper life within you. Most people never truly explore this terrain. They skim along the surface, content with what they can see, assuming that what is hidden must not matter. Yet what is hidden shapes everything. The psyche is not a small thing. It is vast, layered, intricate. It is the secret theatre where every role you have ever played is still alive, and every part of you that you have disowned is still waiting to return.

I have often described the psyche as having its own architecture. Not made of walls and ceilings, but of layers and patterns, each one serving a purpose, each one alive. At the very surface lies what you call your conscious mind. This is the part that makes choices, speaks words, reads these lines now. It is what you normally call "me." It believes it is in control, and in a sense it is, but only in a limited way. Beneath it lies the personal unconscious, a great storehouse of memories, experiences, and emotions that you have long forgotten or pushed aside. And deeper still lies the collective unconscious, something that does not belong only to you but to all of us, a reservoir of shared human experience that stretches back through the centuries. To enter this level is to encounter something both intimate and universal.

The collective unconscious holds what I called archetypes, universal patterns of behaviour and experience that shape the way we live, even when we are unaware of them. These archetypes are not simply images, they are forces. They press upon us, they move through us, they colour our thoughts and shape our dreams. Think of the hero who goes out to conquer and sacrifice, the mother who nurtures and protects, the wise old man who guides, the trickster who deceives and disrupts. These figures appear in myths from every culture, in the stories of every age, because they live in us as potentials. They rise in our fantasies, they appear in our art, they echo in our religions. They are not invented by us, we are born into them.

When you dream, when you watch a story unfold, something within you recognises it. That recognition is the archetype speaking. When you feel drawn to a hero's struggle or moved by a mother's sacrifice, it is not only empathy, it is resonance. You are meeting your own inner patterns. Archetypes are not meant to imprison you, they are meant to guide you. They show you that you are part of something larger, that your struggles are not merely personal but human.

Above these deeper forces lies the mask you wear, what I called the Persona. The Persona is the face you show to the world. You wear it at work, at home, with friends, even with yourself. It is the role you have learned to play to be accepted. Without it you would feel too exposed, too vulnerable. But the danger is that you come to believe the mask is your true face. You begin to identify with it completely, forgetting that it is only a role. The Persona is useful, but it is not you. It is a survival tool, a social necessity, but it is not the full truth of who you are.

Behind the Persona lies the Shadow. The Shadow is everything you were told not to be, everything you learned was unacceptable. Anger, jealousy, greed, fear, shame, but also gifts that frightened others, creativity that was dismissed, sensitivity that was mocked, ambition that was labelled selfish. All of this retreated into the dark. The Shadow is not evil. It is exiled. It is everything that has been pushed away, waiting to be seen again. You may think you have buried it, but it will not stay silent. It will rise in your anger, in your projections, in the qualities you despise most in others. You may think you hate arrogance in someone else, when in truth you have denied your own longing to be seen. You may condemn laziness in another, when in truth you have banished your own need for rest. The Shadow is cunning. It shows itself in disguise, but if you pay attention, you will see it everywhere.

Beyond the Shadow live two powerful forces, the Anima and Animus. These are the inner feminine and masculine energies that shape how you love, how you relate, how you balance yourself. A man may repress his softness, his vulnerability, his intuition, and then project them onto a woman, expecting her to carry what he has denied in himself. A woman may repress her assertiveness, her authority, her clarity, and then project them onto a man, expecting him to carry her hidden strength. These inner figures are not problems to be solved but bridges to be crossed. They remind us that we are not half but whole, that within us lives both strength and tenderness, clarity and compassion. To meet them is to reclaim the missing half of your soul.

And at the very centre lies the Self, the deepest truth of who you are. The Self is not the ego, not the little "I" that thinks it directs everything. The Self is the totality of you, the wholeness that holds both your conscious and unconscious, your known and unknown. It is the greater you that calls you to become whole. Individuation, the journey of becoming yourself, is nothing less than the unfolding of the Self. To ignore it is to remain divided, restless, incomplete. To follow it is to feel the quiet pull of meaning, the sense that your life has a purpose beyond survival.

This structure is not a theory alone. It is alive in you right now. Your Persona is at work whenever you put on a smile you do not feel, whenever you say yes when you want to say no. Your Shadow stirs whenever you feel an irrational irritation, whenever you overreact, whenever you catch yourself judging harshly. The Anima and Animus whisper in your longings, in your relationships, in your attractions and projections. And the Self waits, always calling you towards integration. This is not abstract, it is lived. It is present in every decision you make, every dream you dream, every fear you feel.

You may wonder why this matters. Why should you explore this inner architecture? Because without it, you are not fully alive. To live only on the surface is to walk through life half-asleep. You may succeed, you may achieve, you may be admired, but you will not know yourself. And without knowing yourself, every achievement will feel hollow. You will chase recognition, approval, wealth, love, but none of it will quiet the inner ache. The ache comes from neglecting the Self. It comes from pretending that your shadow does not exist, from believing your Persona is your true identity, from ignoring the archetypes that move within you.

To know yourself is not to control everything, but to listen. It is to notice the patterns, to recognise the masks, to honour the shadow, to welcome the Anima and Animus, to follow the quiet voice of the Self. It is to accept that you are not only light, not only dark, but both, and that both are needed. The psyche is not chaos. It has order, it has meaning, it has purpose. But it demands that you pay attention.

I cannot promise that the journey inward will be easy. It will not. To face the shadow is to face fear, shame, guilt, wounds you would rather keep buried. To meet the Anima or Animus is to confront parts of yourself that unsettle you. To follow the Self is to walk away from the expectations of others, to risk becoming truly yourself. Yet this is the only journey worth taking. To refuse it is to remain divided. To accept it is to become whole.

The psyche is alive within you. It speaks in your dreams, in your slips of the tongue, in your sudden emotions. It appears in your art, in your stories, in your myths. It whispers in every quiet moment, asking you to listen. You are not only who you think you are. You are more. And until you recognise that more, you will remain restless.

So listen now. Feel the pull of the Self. Notice the weight of the Persona, the whisper of the Shadow, the stirrings of the archetypes. They are not outside you. They are you. And to know them is to know yourself.

Chapter 3

Persona, Shadow, & the Masks We Wear

When I look back on my own life, I cannot help but see how many times I wore a mask and pretended it was my face. I wore it as a child when I wanted the approval of my father, I wore it as a student when I wanted to be seen as clever among my peers, I wore it as a doctor when I wanted to be regarded as reliable and steady. The truth is that every one of us has done the same. We put on a mask without even noticing, because life seems to demand it of us. It is not always malicious, it is survival. A child learns quickly which behaviours please and which bring punishment, so they hide certain parts and exaggerate others. By the time they are grown, they may not even remember what is genuine beneath the role. I was no exception.

The Persona, as I came to call it, is that carefully chosen disguise we wear when facing the world. It is the voice you adopt in the office, the polite laugh you offer at a dinner party, the firm handshake, the mask of competence or charm or modesty. It can be useful, it can help you survive and even thrive, but it is still a mask. The danger is not in wearing it, but in believing that the mask is all you are. When that happens, you become a ghost of yourself, living out roles for others while something inside you quietly withers.

I remember the first time I truly saw my own Persona. I was a young psychiatrist, eager to impress, hungry for recognition. In those early years I played the role of the brilliant student, the promising doctor, the loyal follower of Freud. It was a mask that fitted me well, and for a time I believed it. Yet I noticed something strange. In private moments, when the mask was not needed, I felt restless. I felt as though my own skin did not fit. I was anxious, irritable, filled with vague dissatisfaction. I began to understand that the Persona, for all its usefulness, could also become a prison. It was like a stage costume I had worn for so long that I could no longer remember what my real clothes felt like.

Behind the Persona waits the Shadow, and here is where the story becomes uncomfortable. For the Shadow is everything you and I have pushed away. It is the anger we were told was inappropriate, the desires we were shamed for, the weaknesses we were mocked for, the selfishness we were scolded for. But it is also more than this. It contains gifts that frightened others, tenderness that was dismissed as weakness, creativity that was discouraged, ambition that was punished. When I first began to encounter my Shadow, I did not greet it kindly. I recoiled, as most people do. For I found there not only anger and jealousy, but arrogance, lust, fear, cowardice. I found parts of myself I did not want to admit existed.

There was a time when I prided myself on my rationality, on my ability to analyse and control. Yet in dreams I was confronted with figures that terrified me. They were grotesque, violent, sometimes obscene. They disturbed me so deeply that I wanted to dismiss them. But I could not. They returned night after night, pressing upon me with an authority that reason could not silence. It was then I began to understand that the Shadow does not disappear simply because we pretend it does not exist. In fact, the more we repress it, the stronger it becomes. The Shadow thrives in darkness. It grows in the places where we refuse to look.

I saw it too in my patients. A man who hated dishonesty was later revealed to be lying to himself about his own affairs. A woman who despised greed in others was hiding a desperate hunger for love and recognition. A child who was punished for being angry became an adult who smiled sweetly but exploded in sudden rages.

Projection, I came to call it. What we deny in ourselves, we cannot help but see in others. It is a strange mirror, cruel at times, but it is also the way the unconscious reveals what we have tried to bury.

I am not immune to this. I once found myself deeply irritated by a colleague, convinced he was pompous and self-important. Only later, in a quiet moment of painful honesty, did I see that I too carried that same pompous streak. I had hidden it from myself, but the world has a way of showing us our shadows through the people we least wish to resemble. It is humbling, sometimes humiliating, but it is necessary. Without those mirrors, we would remain blind.

The Shadow is not only made of what we despise. It also carries what we long for but fear to embrace. How many men, afraid of being seen as weak, hide their tenderness until it becomes bitterness? How many women, afraid of being seen as unfeminine, hide their strength until it becomes resentment? Within the Shadow live not only our demons but our lost treasures. To deny it is to cut off parts of our own soul. To embrace it is to become more whole.

When I began to truly work with my Shadow, I realised how much of my life had been dictated by fear of being seen. I had worn the Persona of the doctor, the scholar, the loyal colleague, and each had served me. Yet behind them all was a longing I had not allowed myself to fully feel: the longing to know, to explore the depths of the human soul even if it meant walking away from accepted paths. That longing frightened me, for it risked rejection, ridicule, even exile from the world I depended on. And indeed, when I broke with Freud, it felt as though the ground beneath me collapsed. The mask I had worn as his disciple was ripped away, and I was left raw, exposed, uncertain of who I was. Yet it was in that very exposure that I began to discover myself.

You may know this feeling too. Perhaps you have lived as the dutiful child, the good employee, the agreeable friend, and one day you feel a restlessness you cannot explain. You begin to notice that the role no longer fits. You feel suffocated, unseen, trapped. That is your Shadow pressing against the Persona, demanding to be heard. It is painful, even terrifying, but it is also the beginning of freedom.

What happens if you refuse to listen? Then the Shadow will find other ways. It may erupt in sudden anger, in destructive behaviour, in illness, in depression. It may sabotage your relationships, your work, your peace. The Shadow does not vanish when ignored, it only grows stronger. Many of the crises we face in midlife are nothing less than the Shadow demanding entry into consciousness. We call it a breakdown, but it is often a breakthrough. The mask has cracked, and what was hidden now demands to be integrated.

To integrate the Shadow does not mean to indulge it. It does not mean to give free rein to every dark impulse. It means to recognise it, to accept that it exists, to find a way to give it expression without destruction. When I felt arrogance rise in me, I could not simply deny it. I had to ask: in what way can this arrogance be a teacher? Perhaps it is a call to own my strength more honestly, rather than hiding behind false modesty. When I felt anger, I had to ask: where is the injustice that needs to be named? When I felt fear, I had to ask: what task is waiting for me on the other side of this fear?

This work is not comfortable. It will ask you to admit things you would rather deny. It will strip away illusions you have clung to. It will humble you again and again. And yet, as I have found, it will also set you free. For every mask you remove, every shadow you embrace, brings you closer to your true self.

Sometimes I imagine it like this: the Persona is a house you build on a busy street, painted neatly, decorated to please the neighbours. It looks impressive, respectable. But in the basement lies a door you never open. Behind that door is the Shadow, waiting. At first you keep it locked and convince yourself the house above is enough. But the Shadow begins to rattle the door. It leaks into the house in strange noises, in flickering lights, in cracks in the walls. You can pretend for a time, but eventually you must go down and open that door. And when you do, you find not only darkness but forgotten treasures. Rooms you did not know you had. Strength you did not know you carried. Beauty you had long abandoned. The house becomes larger, truer, more alive.

This is why I speak so personally about the Persona and the Shadow. For I too have walked through those doors, trembling, reluctant, ashamed. I too have faced parts of myself I wanted to keep hidden. I too have felt the terror of removing the mask and not knowing who would remain. And I tell you this: the one who remains is more real, more whole, more alive than any mask could ever be.

So let me ask you now: what mask do you wear each day? Whose approval are you still seeking? What qualities in others stir your deepest irritation? And could it be that those same qualities are alive in you, waiting to be seen? The answers will not come easily, but they will come. And when they do, you will find yourself not diminished but enlarged, not shamed but liberated.

The Persona kept me safe, but it also kept me small. The Shadow frightened me, but it also led me home. And perhaps that is the paradox we must all live. To be fully human is to be both mask and shadow, light and dark, accepted and hidden. But to become truly ourselves, we must risk taking off the mask, opening the door, and welcoming every part of who we are.

The Growing Practice of Shadow Work

Chapter 4

Naming the Darkness

There was a time in my life when I was afraid of my own mind. Not the thoughts that passed through it, but the deeper impulses, the strange eruptions of feeling that seemed to arrive from nowhere, uninvited. I would sit at my desk, writing or reading, and suddenly be seized by a wave of rage at some long-forgotten slight, or by a craving that embarrassed me, or by an image in a dream so unsettling that I dared not describe it to anyone. I told myself it was nothing, that I was above such childish impulses. But the truth is, those impulses were mine. They belonged to me as much as my intellect or my skills. And until I dared to name them, they ruled me from the shadows.

That is the thing about darkness. It does not disappear simply because we refuse to look at it. It waits, it lingers, it whispers. It grows heavy in the corners of the psyche until it finds a way to break free, sometimes in the most destructive of ways. You know this already. Perhaps you have lost your temper over something small, only to wonder later why you exploded. Perhaps you have felt envy so sharp it cut you, though you would never admit it aloud. Perhaps you have found yourself judging someone harshly, only to sense, in the back of your mind, that you were judging in them what you cannot face in yourself.

I have done all these things. I remember sitting across from a patient, nodding with professional calm while inside me there was a small, mean voice mocking their fears. Where did that voice come from? It was mine, though I wished it were not. I judged myself for it, hated myself for it, and yet it returned. Only when I began to write in my private journals, unguarded, unfiltered, did I see it clearly. It was not just mockery. It was my own fear of weakness, my own shame about my vulnerability, projected onto those I claimed to help. To name that darkness was painful. It shattered the image I had of myself as noble and compassionate. But once it was named, it began to loosen its hold.

Naming the darkness does not mean you parade it before the world. It means you admit it to yourself, in the quiet honesty of your own heart. I have had to name my anger, my pride, my jealousy, my cowardice. Each one felt like swallowing fire. I would write them in my notebook, my hand shaking as though the words themselves burned: I am arrogant. I am afraid. I am envious. I crave recognition. I long for things I dare not speak. These confessions tore at me. And yet, in naming them, I found a strange kind of relief. The monster in the dark became smaller once I dared to shine a light on it.

You will find this too. What you most fear to name is often what most needs to be spoken. Perhaps you carry resentment towards your parents, though you tell yourself you are grateful. Perhaps you envy your friends' successes, though you smile and congratulate them. Perhaps you lust, though you pretend purity. Perhaps you are terrified of failure, though you posture as confident. These are not sins to be eradicated. They are truths to be acknowledged. They are part of you, whether you wish it or not. And until you name them, they will twist your life in secret.

When I began to teach this work, I would tell my students and patients to imagine a newspaper headline: The Worst Things About You. What would it say? That you are selfish? Weak? Dishonest? Lazy? Needy? Write them down. Let them sting. Let them breathe. The more it hurts, the more you know you are close to your shadow. And once the words are there on the page, they lose some of their poison. They no longer hide in silence, waiting to ambush you. They are seen. They are spoken. And in that speaking, they begin to soften.

Dreams too have named my darkness in ways my waking mind would never allow. I have seen my shadow appear as grotesque strangers, as threatening animals, as broken versions of myself. Once, in a dream, I met a hunchbacked man with a twisted face who followed me everywhere. I awoke shaken, repulsed. But I forced myself to ask: who is he? What part of me does he represent? Slowly I saw that he was my shame, the part of me I wanted no one to see. For weeks he haunted my dreams until I finally acknowledged him, until I said aloud, Yes, you are mine too. Only then did the dreams relent.

It is tempting to believe that by naming the darkness we make it worse, that giving it words will give it power. But the opposite is true. What remains unnamed festers. What is named can be integrated. When you whisper, I am jealous, jealousy no longer has to masquerade as righteousness. When you confess, I am afraid, fear no longer needs to disguise itself as anger. When you admit, I want to be seen, that longing no longer drives you to sabotage yourself. To name is to disarm.

I will not lie to you. This naming will break your illusions. It will humble you. It may make you cry. It may make you feel less noble, less pure, less admirable. But it will also make you more real. And in the end, reality is kinder than fantasy. A false image demands constant defence. The truth, once faced, begins to free you.

There is one more thing I must confess. Even after years of studying the mind, even after decades of writing about the shadow, I still find it difficult to name my own darkness. I still resist, still squirm, still reach for excuses. It never becomes easy. But it does become familiar. And with familiarity comes courage. Courage to write it down, to say it aloud in prayer, to admit it to a trusted friend. Each time I do, I feel a little more whole.

So I will ask you, as I ask myself: what do you most fear to admit? What is the word that burns on your tongue but never escapes?

Write it now. Whisper it if you dare. Let it pierce you. That is where your work begins.

In the end, naming the darkness is not about shaming yourself. It is about becoming honest. It is about standing in front of the mirror without the mask, without the excuses, and saying, This too is me. And when you can do that, you will begin to notice something unexpected. The darkness is not only ugly. It is also tender. It carries not only your flaws but your neglected gifts. In the same place where you find your rage, you may also find your passion. In the same place where you find your fear, you may also find your courage. In the same place where you find your envy, you may also find your longing for growth.

To name the darkness is to discover that it is not your enemy. It is your teacher. And once you name it, it can begin to teach you.

Chapter 5

Dreams That Speak

There are nights when I close my eyes and I feel the door open. It is not the door to sleep, though sleep carries me into it, but the door to something far older, far stranger, something that knows me more intimately than I know myself. I have learned to listen when this door opens, for it is in these hours of darkness that the mind begins to speak in its own language. That language is the dream.

I have often felt that dreams are the truest conversations we have with ourselves. By day we wear our masks, we behave, we pretend. We say what is acceptable, we silence what is not. But in the dream world, the silenced parts come alive. They dress themselves as figures, landscapes, animals, sometimes grotesque, sometimes luminous, always carrying a message. And though I spent years trying to dismiss them, I now confess that my dreams have been my greatest teachers.

There was a period in my life, in the years when I broke away from Freud, when my dreams became relentless. They filled my nights with visions that disturbed me so deeply I would wake drenched in sweat, my heart racing, sometimes unable to return to sleep at all. At first I feared I was losing my sanity. I even considered whether the very work I was doing, plunging so deep into the psyche, was undoing me. But slowly, painfully, I realised these dreams were not madness. They were messages. They were the unconscious demanding to be heard.

One dream returned to me often. I would find myself in a house, familiar yet unsettling. At first glance it seemed like my own home, but as I explored it, I found it stretched into rooms I had never seen, corridors that descended underground. Down there, in the basement, I discovered ancient chambers, filled with bones, primitive tools, and traces of lives long gone. It was terrifying, yet magnetic. I knew this house was me. The upper rooms were my conscious life, my daily persona. The lower chambers were my unconscious, the forgotten layers of history within me, and perhaps within all of us. The dream was showing me the architecture of the psyche, layer upon layer, conscious and unconscious, personal and collective.

That dream changed me. It reminded me that we are not simply what we present to the world. We are far older, far stranger, connected to myths and ancestors we cannot remember. Our unconscious is not merely a bin of forgotten memories, it is a living archive, and dreams are its voice.

You may think your own dreams are nonsense, fragments of your day stitched together in confusion. But I tell you, within those fragments lies the map of your soul. A nightmare of falling is not merely fear, but a symbol of insecurity, a cry from the part of you that feels groundless. A dream of being chased is not only terror, but the pursuit of what you avoid in waking life, a demand to face what you flee. A dream of flight is not just fantasy, but the reminder that somewhere inside you longs for freedom.

When I was a boy, I dreamt often of falling into dark water. I would wake in panic, gasping. Only much later did I realise these dreams were about the pull of the unconscious, the waters that awaited me, the plunge I would spend my life exploring. As a man, I dreamt of meeting dark figures who threatened me, mocked me, frightened me. At first I thought they were demons. In time I saw they were my shadow, the very parts of myself I had not yet dared to accept. Each dream was a mirror, though the reflection was disguised.

It is not easy to face these images. I recall vividly the dream in which I saw myself standing on a field while a gigantic wave approached. I ran, I hid, I tried to wake, but I could not escape. The wave crashed over me, and in its water I saw countless faces, as though humanity itself was carried in its tide. That dream shook me. I understood then what I would later call the collective unconscious, the ocean beneath all of us, filled with archetypes, with shared patterns, with symbols older than civilisation. The wave was my fear, but it was also my initiation. I was not just Carl Jung, the individual, I was a vessel of the collective. Dreams remind us of this truth. They tell us we are never entirely alone, for in the images that come to us at night, we see reflections of the myths and stories of all humankind.

I know some will say, but my dreams make no sense. I tell you, sense is not the point. Dreams speak in metaphor, in symbol, in poetry. They bypass the rational mind because reason cannot always bear the truth. A dream dresses your shame as a stranger, your rage as a wild animal, your longing as a distant lover. They disguise, because if they revealed themselves too plainly, you would recoil. And yet, once you learn to listen, to ask, What part of me is this figure? What part of me speaks through this image?, then slowly, the meaning unfolds.

I confess to you that I resisted this for years. I wanted my mind to be neat, logical, obedient. But life is not neat. The psyche is not obedient. It will speak, whether we wish it or not. Ignore your dreams and they will return, louder, darker, demanding your attention. Welcome them, and they become guides.

There is a humility in this. Dreams remind me that I am not in control. They show me my arrogance, my blind spots, my wounds. More than once I have been humbled by a dream that stripped me bare. I have seen myself as weak, as cowardly, as vain. I have seen myself as cruel. And though I woke ashamed, I also woke freer, because the truth, once faced, is less dangerous than the lie.

Let me tell you something more personal. In my journals I kept for myself alone, I wrote down dreams I never spoke of. Dreams of passion, of desire, of violence. Dreams that scandalised me. In daylight, I was respectable. In sleep, I was confronted with instincts and impulses I pretended did not exist. Those dreams taught me compassion. For how could I judge others, when I knew what lived within me? How could I pretend to be above human frailty, when my own unconscious laid it before me night after night? Dreams strip away the mask. They make hypocrites honest. And though it is painful, it is holy work.

I believe your dreams are speaking to you, even now. Perhaps you have dismissed them, perhaps you cannot remember them, perhaps you laugh them off. But I ask you, begin to listen. Keep a notebook by your bed. When you wake, write whatever fragments remain, no matter how small. Do not censor, do not edit. Write the nonsense, the strange, the shameful. With time, you will see the patterns. You will hear the voice beneath the images. And in that voice you will begin to recognise yourself.

Remember this: the dream is not against you. Even your nightmares are not punishments. They are revelations. They show you where you are wounded, where you are hiding, where you are longing. They are not sent to torment, but to guide. The unconscious does not waste its breath. If it speaks, it is because something matters.

I will confess one last thing. Even now, after all my years of studying and honouring dreams, they still unsettle me. They still shake me to my core. And I am glad for it. For each dream is a reminder that I am alive, that I am not finished, that there are still parts of me unknown. And in the unknown, there is life.

So tonight, when you close your eyes, remember this: the door may open. And if it does, do not be afraid. Step through. Let the dream speak. It is your shadow, your longing, your Self calling. And if you dare to listen, you may find that in the darkness of night, you are finally being shown the truth of who you are.

Chapter 6

Archetypes Alive Within

There are times when I have felt less like a man and more like a stage, and upon that stage figures have appeared, played their parts, and vanished again, only to return in another guise. I did not invent them. I did not call for them. Yet they were there, alive within me, shaping my words, my choices, even my silence. These figures are what I have called the archetypes, the patterns of human experience that are older than memory. They do not belong to me alone. They belong to all of us. They are the inheritance of being human, the collective shapes that emerge from the deep well of the unconscious.

At first, I resisted the idea that such forces could truly exist. I told myself I was imagining them, that they were merely poetic language. But the more I studied my dreams, the more I listened to my patients, the more I observed art, myth, and religion across cultures, the more undeniable it became. The same figures returned again and again. The Hero. The Mother. The Wise Old Man. The Trickster. The Anima and Animus, those inner figures of the opposite sex that haunt our relationships. And at the centre of it all, the Self, the wholeness toward which we stumble. They appeared in the dreams of farmers and kings, of children and scholars, of men and women who had never read a book of philosophy. They appeared in ancient myths carved in stone and in the paintings of artists who swore they were simply following inspiration. They appeared in me. And once I allowed myself to see them, I realised they were not mere abstractions. They were alive.

I confess to you that I have been both terrified and enthralled by them. They come uninvited. One night, the shadow stands before me as a dark figure in my dreams, mocking, threatening, showing me my weakness. Another night, the Anima arrives, a mysterious woman, beautiful and merciless, stirring emotions in me I cannot contain. At times, the Wise Old Man has spoken words in dreams that I could never have thought of by day, words that carried truth I had not yet learned. And then there are the trickster figures, the fools and jesters who appear when I am most proud, knocking me from my pedestal with their laughter.

Have you not felt this too? A voice inside you that seems not quite your own, urging you, warning you, seducing you? A recurring image in your dreams that feels as though it comes from somewhere beyond your personal history? A fascination with a certain type of story, a certain type of character, that you cannot explain? These are the archetypes alive within you. You cannot escape them, for they are not outside of you. They are the roots from which your psyche grows.

I remember vividly the first time I felt the Anima take hold of me. I was speaking with a woman, and though the conversation was ordinary, something stirred within me, something far beyond her or me. It was as though I was speaking not only with her, but with the eternal feminine itself, that image of womanhood that lives in the male psyche. I felt captivated, even bewitched, and I knew it was not merely about her, but about what she represented within me. It frightened me, for it made me realise how much of my longing, my desire, my projections were shaped not by reality but by this inner figure. It took me years to disentangle the real women in my life from the Anima I carried within me. And yet, when I finally acknowledged her, when I admitted that this inner figure existed, I began to see more clearly, to love more honestly.

The same has been true of the Trickster. More than once I have been fooled by my own pride. I thought myself wise, only to be undone by a careless mistake. I thought myself superior, only to be humbled by laughter. In those moments I could almost hear the Trickster chuckling, reminding me that seriousness can become a mask, that even the most solemn truths must sometimes be broken by humour. The Trickster is cruel, but he is also liberating. Without him, we would suffocate under our own importance.

And then there is the Mother. She appears not only as our personal mothers, but as the image of nurturance itself, the force of life that carries, feeds, and protects. In dreams, she may appear as a great tree, as the earth itself, as a woman whose arms can hold the world. But she can also appear as the devouring mother, the one who smothers, who consumes, who does not let go. I have seen both in my patients' dreams, and in my own. To recognise her is to recognise our own need to be cared for, and our fear of being consumed.

These archetypes are not fantasies. They are the patterns of life itself. They shape how we love, how we fear, how we grow. When you fall in love, you are not simply seeing another person, you are also seeing your Anima or Animus projected upon them. When you face a great challenge, you are stepping into the Hero's journey, whether you know it or not. When you seek wisdom, you are calling upon the Wise Old Man within you. When you sabotage yourself, when you laugh at the wrong moment, when you make a fool of yourself despite your best efforts, the Trickster is at work.

I do not tell you this to frighten you, but to awaken you. For if you know these forces, if you can name them, then you can work with them instead of being ruled by them. Too many live blind, thinking their desires and fears are purely personal, when in fact they are echoes of something universal. To recognise the archetype in your dream, in your reaction, in your attraction, is to see the thread that connects you to all of humanity. It is humbling, yes, but it is also liberating. You realise you are not alone. Your struggles are not unique failures. They are the patterns of the human story, playing out through you.

I will confess something else. There are times when I feel as though I am only half in control of my own life. The other half belongs to these archetypal forces. They rise in me, they fall away, they return. I do not command them. I can only listen, wrestle, surrender. And in those moments when I have tried to deny them, to insist I am simply myself and nothing more, I have found myself most lost. It is when I admit their presence, when I bow to their reality, that I begin to find balance.

So I urge you, do not dismiss the figures that visit you in your dreams. Do not ignore the patterns in your life that repeat. Do not laugh away the stories that move you to tears. They are not accidents. They are the archetypes alive within you, shaping you, calling you toward wholeness. To know them is to know yourself. To ignore them is to be forever at their mercy.

I have seen men destroyed by their unacknowledged archetypes. A man possessed by the Hero who cannot admit defeat becomes reckless, burning out in glory or ruin. A woman possessed by the Mother who cannot let go consumes those around her in smothering love. A scholar possessed by the Wise Old Man becomes arrogant, blind to his ignorance. A fool possessed by the Trickster loses all direction, turning life into chaos. But I have also seen men and women transformed when they recognise these forces, when they integrate them instead of being ruled. The Hero becomes courage, the Mother becomes nurturance, the Wise Old Man becomes guidance, the Trickster becomes laughter. The Anima and Animus become bridges to deeper love, not prisons of projection. And at the centre, the Self begins to emerge, the wholeness that is not the domination of one archetype but the harmony of them all.

In my own life, I am still learning this. I am still surprised by the figures that appear. I am still humbled by the way they show me what I have ignored. But I no longer deny them. I no longer pretend they are fantasies. They are real, as real as breath, as real as love, as real as fear. And the more I acknowledge them, the more I feel alive, not as a puppet on their strings, but as a man in dialogue with the deepest forces of his own soul.

And so I tell you now, if you wish to know yourself, if you wish to be whole, do not turn away when these figures appear. Welcome them. Listen to them. Wrestle with them. They are your inheritance. They are your companions. They are alive within you, and they always will be.

Chapter 7

Battle Between Light & Dark

There are nights when I have woken in terror, not from any sound outside me, but from the storm within. I have seen myself in dreams standing in a hall divided, one side drenched in shadow, the other radiant with light, and I felt torn between them, unable to belong fully to either. And in the silence of those nights, I knew the truth I wish I could deny: I am not only good, and I am not only evil, but both live within me, and they do not rest.

As a young man, I wanted to be virtuous. I wanted to be seen as honourable, wise, compassionate. I wanted to be a man of light. But the more I tried to live in the light, the more I felt the pull of the darkness at my feet. Anger I could not control. Lust I could not admit. Envy I could not bear to acknowledge. Cruelty in the thoughts I tried to bury. I felt ashamed of these things, and so I fought them. I tried to silence them, to smother them under piety, under philosophy, under respectability. But the more I fought, the stronger they grew. It was as though, in denying them, I fed them.

I remember once sitting across from a patient, speaking gently, calmly, presenting myself as a figure of compassion. And inside, another voice was mocking them, cruel and cutting. That voice was mine. It shamed me. It broke my image of myself. I went home that night and sat in silence, asking, who am I really? The healer, or the hypocrite? The truth, of course, is both. I am both. And the war between them is unending.

I have seen this war in myself, but I have also seen it in every soul I have ever known. The man who preaches kindness yet lashes out in rage at his children. The woman who appears gentle but secretly seethes with envy. The priest who prays in public but hides his hunger in private. The warrior who kills with bravery and then weeps in shame. Light and dark, woven into every being. The mistake is to think we can choose only one. The greater truth is that we carry both, always, and the task is not to eliminate the darkness, but to face it, to learn from it, to live with it without letting it consume us.

I confess that there are moments when I have wanted to give in to the darkness entirely. There is a strange seduction in it, a kind of freedom. To stop pretending, to stop striving, to surrender to the rage, the lust, the cruelty. There is a power in it. I felt it once when I struck another boy as a child, struck him harder than I intended, and for a moment I felt triumph, control, mastery. And then I felt horror. The darkness gives, but it also takes. It offers a crown, but it costs your soul. I have seen men surrender to it fully, and they are destroyed. But I have also seen men deny it completely, and they are equally destroyed, broken by the shadow they refuse to acknowledge.

Light too has its dangers. To live only in light, to strive only for purity, can make one brittle, prideful, blind to one's own hypocrisy. I have seen saints whose smiles hid poison, martyrs whose sacrifice was as much about vanity as it was about virtue. To live only in light is to become untouchable, but also unhuman.

The greatest danger of the light is to forget your own shadow, to believe yourself above it. That is when it rises to strike you down.

In me, the battle is constant. I wake in the morning and feel the pull toward goodness, toward work, toward compassion. And by midday I am angry, resentful, impatient. By evening I feel ashamed, and by night I am haunted by dreams where my shadow takes form, mocking me, showing me the parts of myself I pretend not to see. And still I rise the next day, still I return to the work, because I know there is no end. The battle is not to be won. It is to be lived.

I tell you this because you too know it, though perhaps you do not speak of it. You have felt the temptation to lie, even when you preach honesty. You have felt the urge to betray, even as you promise fidelity. You have wanted to harm, even as you declare love.

This is not proof that you are evil. It is proof that you are human. The war between light and dark is the very condition of humanity. To pretend otherwise is to live a lie.

I have learned, painfully, that the task is not to kill the darkness, but to bring it into relationship with the light. My anger can destroy, but it can also give me courage to defend. My lust can degrade, but it can also remind me of the sacredness of union. My envy can corrode, but it can also reveal my hidden desires, what I truly long for. My cruelty can wound, but in recognising it, I can become more compassionate, less quick to judge. The darkness is not to be eradicated. It is to be integrated, balanced by the light, transformed by it, and in turn, giving the light its depth.

I confess, though, that I still fear my own darkness. There are nights when I dream of committing acts so vile I wake shaking, ashamed to even write them in my journal. And yet, when I force myself to put the words on paper, to admit them even to myself, I feel a strange relief. I see then that these dreams are not commands, but warnings, reminders of what lives in me, of what I must remain vigilant against. The darkness shows me my limits, my dangers, my weaknesses. Without it, I would be arrogant. With it, I am humbled.

The light too humbles me. For in those rare moments when I have felt grace, when I have glimpsed something holy in a dream, or in a patient's breakthrough, or in the eyes of someone I love, I have known that goodness is not my possession either. It too is a gift, a force greater than me. I cannot command it any more than I can command the darkness. Both come to me, both live in me, both shape me. And my task is to hold them, not to destroy one in favour of the other, but to let them dance, to let them fight, to let them teach me.

There is a passage I wrote long ago, and it remains true: one does not become enlightened by imagining figures of light, but by making the darkness conscious. Light without darkness is fantasy. Darkness without light is despair. Only in their union is there wholeness.

I will tell you something else, something perhaps I should not. In the years of war, I saw what happens when men surrender to their darkness, when entire nations are swept away by it. I saw cruelty on a scale that shattered me, and I knew then that the battle within each of us is the same battle that plays out in the world. What we repress in ourselves returns as horror in our societies. The tyrant outside is born of the tyrant inside. The violence of nations begins with the violence of men against their own shadows. If we do not face our inner darkness, it will spill outward, and the world will pay the price.

So I ask you, do not pretend you are only light. Do not despair that you are also dark. Stand in the tension between them. Admit your cruelty, your lust, your envy, your rage. Admit also your compassion, your tenderness, your longing for goodness. Let them both speak. Let them both teach you. The battle is not a curse. It is the very ground of your becoming.

As for me, I will go on wrestling. I will go on confessing. I will go on listening to my dreams, naming my shadows, honouring my glimpses of light. I will go on standing in the hall where both shadow and light fall upon me, and I will go on choosing, not once, but every day, every moment. For this is what it means to be human. Not to be pure. Not to be perfect. But to live, always, in the battle between light and dark, and to find in that struggle the path toward wholeness.

Chapter 8

The Steps of Integration

I resisted this chapter for longer than I'd like to admit. Integration is not glamorous, and it is not tidy. It is not a sudden revelation that bursts through the clouds and leaves you glowing with certainty. It is slower, rawer, and often painfully ordinary. It happens in kitchen sinks and quiet walks, in awkward conversations where you hear yourself say something you didn't mean to say, and then you realise it is the shadow speaking. It happens when you wake from a dream that unsettles you and you write it down instead of pushing it away.

I once thought integration meant victory - that I would conquer my flaws, silence my rage, or tidy away the pettiness that embarrassed me. But Jung never spoke of conquest. He spoke of acceptance, of bringing what was hidden into the light so it no longer ruled us from the dark. And that, I learned, is the first step.

Step One: Naming Without Shame

It begins when you name the thing you fear most in yourself. For me, it was jealousy. I hated it, denied it, wrapped it in layers of righteousness so I could pretend it was not there. But jealousy would still seep out - in side comments, in private resentments, in the way I withdrew from people who had the courage to live more boldly than I did. The turning point came when I wrote the words in my journal, "I am jealous." Just that. I felt sick writing it. I wanted to cross it out. Yet the truth of it broke something open. Integration begins with naming without shame.

Step Two: Listening Rather Than Silencing

After naming comes listening. I used to silence the voice inside me that carried my darker impulses. I thought discipline was about suppression. But the more I pushed away anger, or lust, or despair, the louder they grew. Listening changed everything. I asked myself, "What are you trying to tell me?" and then I waited. Anger told me where I had been crossed, where my boundaries were trampled. Envy told me what I secretly longed for but was too timid to claim. Fear told me where my edge was, the very place I was called to grow. The second step is listening with patience, not hurrying to fix, just letting the shadow speak.

Step Three: Tracing the Root

If the shadow is a plant growing wild, its roots reach deep into childhood soil. I remember sitting at the dinner table as a boy, told not to cry, told to swallow my disappointment and be strong. My shadow learned early that tears were weakness, that tenderness was shameful. Decades later, I would find myself unable to comfort a friend because her tears made me squirm. That is how repression works: the root goes unseen until it strangles you. Integration means tracing the root, following the thread back to its origin. Jung always insisted that the shadow is ancient and personal both - a knot of our private past and the collective myths we inherit. To trace the root is to admit, "This did not begin with me, but it lives in me."

Step Four: Speaking the Dialogue

This step frightened me most. Jung called it active imagination. To speak directly with the shadow, to give it form and voice, felt dangerous. I feared it would overtake me. But one night, I sat in silence and wrote as though the jealous part of me were answering my questions. What it wrote was painful and true. It said, "You ignore me, but I know what you want. I know you crave to be seen." That voice was not my enemy. It was a neglected part of me. Dialogue with the shadow is the fourth step. It makes the unknown known.

Step Five: Weaving Into the Whole

The final step is not neat. It is not once-and-done. It is weaving. I did not "solve" jealousy. I did not erase anger. But I learned to say, "You are part of me, and I will use you with care." Anger became my fuel for justice. Jealousy became my compass pointing to unclaimed desires. Fear became my teacher of courage. This is what Jung meant by individuation - not purity, not perfection, but wholeness. To integrate the shadow is to weave it back into the fabric of the self, where it belongs.

These steps are not a ladder you climb once. They are more like a spiral you return to, again and again.

Each season of life reveals new shadows, or old ones in disguise. But the rhythm is the same: name, listen, trace, dialogue, weave. Each time you do, the grip of the unconscious loosens, and you take back a little more of your life.

I confess, sometimes I hate this process. I hate the mirror it holds up. Yet I know that without it, I am a puppet of what I refuse to see. With it, I am at least awake. That, perhaps, is the gift of Jung's shadow work. It does not make us saints. It makes us whole.

Chapter 9

Active Imagination & Dialogue with the Shadow

I remember the first time I tried to speak to the shadow. It felt foolish, almost childish, as though I were playing a game of make-believe. I sat alone in a quiet room, pen in hand, and whispered into the silence, "Who are you?" No answer came, not at first. Only the sound of my own breathing, the faint hum of the refrigerator in the next room, the creak of the chair beneath me. But then, as if something shifted in the air, a voice stirred. It was not loud, not external, but it was unmistakably not my usual voice of reason either. It was sharp, almost mocking. It said, "I am the one you avoid."

That moment shook me. For years I had read about Jung's technique of active imagination, the way he invited his patients to sit quietly, to let the unconscious speak back through image, word, or inner dialogue. I thought I understood the theory. But when it actually happened, when the shadow began to answer me, I felt both terrified and relieved. Terrified because I realised it had been waiting there all along, like a neglected child in the dark. Relieved because now at last I could no longer pretend I was alone in this inner struggle.

Active imagination is not easy. It is not like daydreaming. It is not simply wandering through pleasant fantasies. It is deliberate. It is dangerous at times. You step into the cavern of the unconscious and you call out to what waits in the shadows. Sometimes it comes as a voice. Sometimes as an image, a character, a dream that unfolds while you are awake. And sometimes it comes as silence, which can be just as unnerving.

When I first began, my dialogues were clumsy. I would sit with a notebook and force the words, scribbling questions and then answering them as though I were someone else. It felt contrived. But with practice, I learned to soften, to let the responses rise rather than invent them. And that is where the truth began to show. My shadow told me bluntly what I had been unwilling to admit: that my pursuit of perfection was nothing more than fear dressed up in virtue. That my desire to please others was a mask concealing resentment. That I loved control more than freedom. These confessions did not come from my rational mind. They came from that hidden voice, the one I had pushed away for too long.

The shadow does not flatter you. It does not speak kindly, not at first. It exposes, accuses, sometimes ridicules. I remember once writing a question, "What do you want from me?" and the answer that came back in my own handwriting was, "To stop pretending." I stared at the words for a long time. My hand had written them, yes, but they felt as though they belonged to another presence altogether. That is the unnerving power of active imagination. You open the door to what you deny, and you let it speak.

But here is the strange mercy: once the shadow is allowed to speak, it softens. The neglected child becomes less hostile when you finally look at it. I discovered this one evening when, after pages of accusation, the voice grew quieter. I asked, "Why are you always angry with me?" And it said, "Because you never listen." The truth of it broke me. I wept, not because I was defeated, but because I realised I had been deaf to myself. The anger was not evil. It was abandoned.

Jung often warned that active imagination should be approached with caution. He believed it was best done with a therapist's guidance. And I agree - it can open doors that some people are not ready to walk through alone. Yet even in my private practice, I found that setting mattered. I would light a candle, close the door, and treat the moment as sacred, not casual. I would ask, "Who wants to speak today?" and then wait, patient, as images began to form. Sometimes it was a stern old man, sometimes a frightened child, sometimes an animal that seemed to carry my wildness. Each encounter was different, but all of them were pieces of me, long forgotten but still alive in the dark.

What startled me most was how much wisdom the shadow carried. Beneath the bitterness, beneath the shame, there was guidance I could not access with my rational mind. Once, during a particularly difficult season, I asked what I should do about a decision that tormented me. The answer came simply: "Stop asking for permission." I knew instantly it was true. My conscious self would never have dared phrase it that way, but the shadow had no such hesitation. It told me the raw thing I needed to hear.

And yet, the shadow is not always right. It is not a perfect oracle. It is still a part of you, shaped by wounds and distortions. Dialogue with the shadow is not about obeying every word it utters. It is about relationship. You listen, you question, you argue if you must. But in the end, you honour the voice that has too long been ignored. This is the work of reconciliation, not surrender.

Some days, the dialogues still frighten me. I close the notebook and wonder if I am mad. Then I remember Jung himself, sitting in his study, speaking with Philemon, the wise figure who appeared in his visions. Jung trusted those inner conversations enough to record them in his Red Book, a private text he guarded for years. If the Godfather of shadow work himself could be brave enough to engage with these presences, then perhaps I am simply following the path he lit.

Active imagination has become, for me, less of a practice and more of a friendship. Awkward, uncomfortable, often demanding, but a friendship nonetheless. I no longer approach my shadow as an enemy. I sit down with it like one sits with an estranged relative, knowing there is pain to be worked through, but also knowing there is family blood between us. The shadow is mine. I cannot cast it out without casting out part of myself.

So I speak, and I listen. Some nights the pages of my journal are filled with arguments. Other nights they are filled with unexpected tenderness. Slowly, painfully, a bridge is being built. I do not know if it will ever be complete. Perhaps it is not meant to be. Perhaps the work is simply to keep building, plank by plank, conversation by conversation, until one day the shadow no longer lurks in the dark but sits openly at the table of my life.

That, I think, is what Jung wanted us to know. The shadow is not to be banished. It is to be heard, respected, even loved. Dialogue is the way. And though it feels foolish at times, though it feels frightening at others, it is the only way I have found to truly make peace with myself.

INDIVIDUATION AND THE SELF

Chapter 10

Individuation & Becoming Whole

It is tempting to imagine that psychology, in its golden beginnings, was a neat affair. Two gentlemen with cigars, sipping coffee in Vienna, sketching theories that would save civilisation. The truth is less civilised. Jung and Freud did not sit as equals in polite conversation; they wrestled, postured, admired, and eventually despised one another in ways that read like a Greek tragedy. Their story is what happens when two immense egos collide - each one convinced he had uncovered the secret blueprint of the human mind.

Freud, of course, believed everything came down to sex. Scratch a dream, a slip of the tongue, a neurosis, and what you would find, according to him, was a repressed desire. Jung nodded at this for a while - how could he not? Freud was the reigning king, the father figure, the man Jung once referred to, embarrassingly, as a "secular saint." But even Jung's reverence had limits. He found Freud's obsession too narrow, too crude. Was the soul really nothing more than a theatre for forbidden appetites? Jung thought not.

Here is where the sarcasm comes in, because one almost pities Freud. He reduced the cathedral of the psyche to a bedroom drama. For him, individuation was not even a concept worth naming. Why bother becoming whole when you could simply unearth your childhood traumas and be done with it? Jung, on the other hand, wanted more. He wanted depth, myth, symbols, meaning. He wanted to bring God back into the conversation - not in a doctrinal way, but as a living reality of the unconscious.

Imagine how that sounded to Freud, who regarded religion as little more than collective neurosis. No wonder their friendship cracked.

And yet, this crack is the birthplace of individuation. When Jung finally tore himself away from Freud's shadow - and make no mistake, Freud was Jung's shadow for years - he entered his own dark night. He was haunted, tormented, even on the brink of madness. He painted, dreamed, recorded visions of gods and demons in his Red Book, not because it was fashionable but because it was survival. Out of that crisis came his greatest insight: that the human being is not meant to be cured into normalcy, but invited into wholeness.

Individuation is not about becoming good. Jung despised the very idea of "goodness" as a final goal. He once said, "I do not wish to be good, I wish to be whole." Wholeness includes light and dark, saint and sinner, wisdom and folly.

This is the offensive part of Jung, the part that makes people squirm. He tells us plainly: you will not be saved by cutting off your flaws like gangrenous limbs. You will be saved - if salvation is the word - by accepting them, learning their place, and folding them into the totality of who you are.

It is almost comical, in a tragic way, how Freud and Jung split on this point. Freud clung to repression as the organising principle: shove down what is dangerous, make it conscious if you must, but always keep it managed. Jung rebelled. He said repression was precisely the problem. What you bury becomes more dangerous. What you ignore becomes what drives you. Wholeness demands the opposite: facing, integrating, enduring the discomfort until the psyche realigns itself around truth rather than denial.

When I think of individuation, I often picture a courtroom. Freud as the stern prosecutor, insisting all roads lead to the libido, and Jung as the defendant who refuses the charge. "No," Jung insists, "we are not mere bundles of instincts. We are mythic creatures. We dream the dreams of our ancestors. We carry gods in our bones." That defiance cost him Freud's friendship, his reputation in some circles, and nearly his sanity. But it also gave birth to the single most daring idea in modern psychology: that the point of life is not success, or happiness, or virtue, but to become your Self, capital S.

Do not mistake this Self for the ego. The ego is a flimsy actor, a mask for social survival. The Self, in Jung's vision, is the whole stage, the audience, the theatre, and the script all at once. It is the total personality, conscious and unconscious, reconciled into one living organism. Individuation is the journey toward that Self - the slow, often humiliating process of becoming the full human you were always meant to be, rather than the convenient fragment society applauds.

Of course, the process is brutal. It is not affirmations and scented candles. It is dreams that terrify you, choices that undo you, failures that expose you. Jung himself endured visions so intense he feared for his sanity. He would later insist that those who cannot bear solitude will never truly individuate. That sounds harsh, almost cruel, but it is true. You cannot meet the Self if you are forever distracted, comforted, entertained. You must face the silence. You must face yourself.

And here is the emotional trigger, the part we all resist: individuation means loss. Loss of illusions, loss of masks, sometimes loss of people who only knew you by the masks you wore. Friends drift, families recoil, careers falter, because the new you no longer plays the old role. Jung called this "the achievement of personality," and it is costly. But the cost of refusing it is greater. To refuse individuation is to remain a half-person, forever haunted by the parts you deny.

Perhaps this is why Freud and Jung could never reconcile. Freud could not abide Jung's mysticism, his insistence on meaning beyond biology. Jung could not tolerate Freud's reductionism, his refusal to admit the soul into psychology. Their feud is etched into the very fabric of modern thought, but beneath the quarrel is a lesson for us: individuation always requires a break. Sometimes from a mentor, sometimes from a culture, sometimes from your own cherished ideals. You must betray in order to be true.

Individuation, then, is rebellion. Not the shallow rebellion of adolescence, but the deep rebellion of the soul claiming its right to exist in full. To individuate is to say: I will not live as a fragment. I will not exile my shadow. I will not accept society's mask as my only face. I will become whole, even if it costs me my comfort, even if it costs me your approval. That is the scandal of Jung, and that is his gift.

Chapter 11

Fear, Failure, & the Tasks That Shape Us

If individuation were simply a matter of choosing wholeness and sticking with it, there would be no problem. A neat syllabus, a tidy checklist: integrate shadow, embrace archetypes, achieve Self, collect certificate on the way out. But Jung never promised anything so bureaucratic. Instead, he promised you terror. He promised you failure. He promised you the kind of tasks that shake your hands, rattle your sleep, and make you wonder whether it might have been easier to stay in Freud's camp, where everything could be explained by sex and childhood tantrums.

The great comedy of the Freud-Jung rivalry is that Freud thought he was protecting people from delusion, while Jung accused him of delusion itself. Freud insisted the unconscious was a cellar of repressed filth; Jung retorted that it was a cathedral of meaning. Freud accused Jung of metaphysical fantasy; Jung thought Freud was frightened, hiding behind his sexual reductionism because he could not bear the full abyss. Each man saw the other as a coward. And perhaps both were right.

Fear, for Jung, was not a problem to be medicated away. Fear was an invitation. "Where your fear is, there is your task," he wrote, and he meant it literally. If a dream terrifies you, follow it. If a thought unsettles you, interrogate it. If you recoil from some truth about yourself, lean in. This was not masochism; it was courage. To him, fear was the compass needle of the soul, always trembling toward the next frontier.

But fear rarely arrives alone. It brings its companion, failure. Individuation is not a polished self-help journey where everything improves on schedule. It is a messy experiment. Jung's own breakdown in the years after his split with Freud was a textbook case: visions of gods and corpses, nights of despair, days where he wandered the edge of psychosis. He failed by every standard of bourgeois success. To his colleagues, he looked unhinged. To his critics, he confirmed their suspicions that his mystical psychology was little more than personal madness dressed up in theory.

And yet, out of that very failure came his greatest insights. The Red Book - that illuminated manuscript of his descent - was not a triumph of mental health; it was the spoils of survival. Jung did not deny that he nearly went under. He admitted it. He confessed it. And in that confession lies the rawest truth of individuation: you cannot become whole without first being broken.

Contrast this with Freud. Freud loathed failure. He built his theories like fortresses, defended them with armies of loyal disciples, excommunicated anyone who dared to question his authority. Freud's fear was not of neurosis - he could write volumes about that - but of his own fragility being exposed. Jung, to his credit, let fragility take centre stage. He allowed himself to be undone. He gambled his reputation on the conviction that collapse could be a doorway. And for that, Freud called him a mystic, a traitor, even a fool.

Perhaps Jung was all three. But he was also right.

Failure is not optional on the path of individuation. It is mandatory. You will betray someone - perhaps yourself, perhaps others. You will lose the mask you thought was your face. You will stumble, sometimes in humiliating ways. And those failures, far from disqualifying you, are the very tasks that shape you. Without them, you remain a fragment. With them, you become a story.

The emotional trigger here is unavoidable: most of us live in terror of failure because we confuse it with death. Lose a job, a relationship, a dream, and it feels like obliteration. Society encourages that fear. It rewards the mask, punishes the crack. It tells us to polish, to brand, to "curate" a self that is always smiling, always competent. Jung spat on that lie. He told us to look into the abyss, to admit our incompetence, our cowardice, our mess. He told us to let the mask fall and trust that something deeper would rise.

This is why Jung still matters, and why Freud, for all his genius, feels increasingly sterile in comparison. Freud explained our weaknesses, but Jung dared us to endure them. Freud gave us the science of management; Jung gave us the art of becoming. One makes you safe. The other makes you alive.

If you want to know what individuation feels like, do not picture enlightenment. Picture humiliation. Picture failing in front of others. Picture nights of anxiety that nobody can soothe. Picture doors closing and your ego howling. Then picture something stranger: the quiet recognition that you are still here. That the failure did not kill you. That the fear did not swallow you. That, on the contrary, you have grown more human because of it.

In the end, Jung was not romantic about this. He knew individuation was dangerous. He knew some would falter. He warned openly that diving into the unconscious without guidance could be destructive. But he also knew that to avoid it altogether was worse. To refuse the call of fear and failure is to calcify into a mask, a persona so rigid it shatters at the first true blow.

So yes, Freud could keep his tidy theories and his loyal circle. Jung chose exile, visions, and failure. Out of that choice came a psychology that dares to tell us: your fear is your teacher, your failure is your initiation, your darkness is your task. If you can bear that, if you can stand in the ruins of your illusions, then individuation is not a myth. It is the beginning of freedom.

Chapter 12

Light & Dark Together – Living Beyond Illusion

If the shadow was merely a curiosity, a dark corner in the attic of the mind, perhaps we could afford to leave it untouched. But Jung insisted it was not some accessory to the psyche - it was central. And what makes him the Godfather of Shadow Work is that he refused to let us play with half a deck. He looked at humanity, at himself, at me, at you, and said, "If you will not embrace both the light and the dark, you are living in illusion."

Freud would have laughed here, a brittle laugh, full of superiority. He would accuse Jung of romanticising the unconscious, gilding pathology into myth. But Freud's fortress never built a bridge. It explained, dissected, reduced - but it never integrated. Jung did something scandalous: he dared to tell us that wholeness means contradiction, that healing requires accepting the very things we want to disown. That is why I call him the Godfather. He baptised the shadow in our psychology, gave it a name, and demanded we respect it.

Living beyond illusion means refusing to play make-believe with our persona. This, I confess, is where I stumbled again and again. When I wrote Activate the Subconscious, I thought I had reached the core of my own being, learning to still my mind, to listen to the whispers beneath the noise. But the shadow is never silent for long. It drummed at the door. It mocked my meditations. It whispered truths I did not want to hear. That is why Shadow Work Demystified was born - not because I had the answers, but because

I was desperate to map the terrain that Jung had already charted, to make the frightening manageable.

But maps are not the same as journeys. Shadow Work Evolution came later, after I had failed enough times to know that no diagram could save me from the night sea journey. Evolution meant learning to live with collapse, to see failure as initiation, to stop trying to kill the shadow and instead ask it to walk beside me. Writing that book, I realised that Jung's greatest gift was not theory - it was the audacity to live his own madness and make it medicine.

And yet, there is still more. Jung did not stop at shadow integration. He led us toward individuation, toward the terrifying possibility that we could become whole. Whole - not good, not perfect, not pure. Whole. That word frightens us more than perfection ever could. Perfection is safe. It allows us to posture, to pretend, to curate. Wholeness is raw. It demands we carry our failures, our jealousies, our hungers, our lusts, our cowardice - and our brilliance, our love, our courage - in the same vessel.

To live beyond illusion is to walk into your own contradictions and bow.

This is not philosophy for its own sake. It is survival. Think of the child who is told never to cry, who learns to silence grief until it bursts out as rage. Think of the woman who is told her ambition is shameful, who hides it until it calcifies into bitterness. Think of the man who is told that tenderness makes him weak, who buries it until he cannot hold love without fear. These are not abstractions - they are the lives we live every day, trapped by illusions of what is acceptable. Jung saw through that lie. He told us the shadow is not your enemy. It is your inheritance.

So when I write now, when I confess, when I hold up Jung's torch and call him the Godfather of Shadow Work, I do it because I have seen the damage of illusions firsthand. I have worn masks so long they burned into my skin. I have denied myself until I was a hollow echo. And every time I tried to chase only the light, I collapsed into darkness. The truth, as Jung forces me to admit, is that the two are inseparable.

The emotional trigger here is sharp: your life is not a problem to be solved, it is a paradox to be lived. Every attempt to amputate the dark side of your being will fail. Every attempt to live in the light alone will rot. And every denial of the shadow is an act of violence against yourself. To be whole is to stand naked in the paradox, trembling but unbroken.

And what comes next - in the modern world, in the culture that pretends it has no shadow - is even more urgent. Because if Jung was right, and if I have learned anything through my own stumbling works, it is this: the collective shadow is no less dangerous than the personal one. Our culture, our politics, our myths, our celebrities, our gods - all of them project the parts we refuse to own. And to live beyond illusion now, we must not only confess individually, we must confess collectively.

That is the task. That is the wound. That is why Jung, the Godfather of Shadow Work, still matters more than ever.

Carl Jung in the Modern World

Chapter 14

Therapy, Self-Practice, & the Risk of Misuse

Here is the bitter truth: Jung gave us a razor, and we have been playing with it like a toy.

Therapy was meant to be the crucible of shadow work - the place where a patient could confront their demons with a guide strong enough to withstand projection and counter-transference. Jung himself said the therapist must have done their own shadow work first, otherwise the therapy collapses into two unconscious minds colliding like drunk dancers. But in the modern world, therapy has been diluted, outsourced, and often commercialised into a sterile transaction.

We have replaced the sacred dialogue with prescription pads, insurance codes, and polite affirmations. This is not shadow work. It is symptom management.

I have seen this danger up close. When I wrote Activate the Subconscious, I spoke of the overstimulated mind and the false promises of productivity culture. People devoured it, nodding along, highlighting passages - but many still wanted a shortcut. They wanted meditation as a sedative, not as a mirror. They wanted calm without confrontation. They wanted the subconscious as a servant, not as a partner. That is not shadow work. That is self-hypnosis dressed as wellness.

Then came Shadow Work Demystified. That book was a plea, an attempt to peel away the glamour and return shadow work to its roots - not a weekend retreat, not a $300 course, but a daily act of brutal honesty. Even then, I knew it would be misused. Some would skim the exercises and declare themselves "healed." Others would cherry-pick the parts that made them feel powerful while ignoring the parts that demanded humility. I wrote it knowing that misuse was inevitable. And it was.

By the time I reached Shadow Work Evolution, the lesson had sunk deep. Evolution is not comfort. Evolution is mutation. It is awkward, painful, dangerous. It costs you friends. It costs you illusions. And it never ends. The risk of misuse here is obvious: people will read the word "evolution" and imagine progress, levelling up, a tidy ascent. But evolution does not move tidily upward. It lurches. It stumbles. It kills what no longer fits. Misuse happens when we demand wholeness on our terms, in our timeline, without sacrifice.

And this is the great trap of modern therapy and self-practice alike: they sell safety when Jung promised danger. To work with the shadow is to risk breakdown. To invite the unconscious into dialogue is to gamble with your ego's survival. This is why Jung warned that not everyone should plunge in without guidance - the psyche can drown as easily as it can rise. Yet the modern world ignores this warning. Journals are sold, apps are downloaded, coaches with no training peddle "shadow work" sessions over Zoom. Misuse flourishes because demand is high and discernment is low.

But here is the emotional trigger I cannot ignore: even in its misused form, shadow work still touches something real. Even when clumsy, it can open a crack. Even when shallow, it can spark a recognition. I cannot condemn people for reaching clumsily toward their own depth - because I did the same. I stumbled, misused, misunderstood, and still I found Jung waiting, patient as ever, torch in hand.

The embarrassment is Freud's. He would say the whole thing is delusion, that we are romanticising neurosis, that self-practice without a trained analyst is folly. He would smirk as untrained seekers stumble. Jung would not smirk. Jung would weep, then insist we go deeper. He would remind us that risk is the very heart of individuation. That without risk, we are not doing shadow work at all.

So yes, misuse is everywhere. Yes, therapy is often too thin, and self-practice often too reckless. But I would rather live in a world fumbling toward Jung's abyss than a world locked in Freud's cellar. Misuse is not the end. It is the beginning. It is the crooked doorway through which countless souls still stumble into wholeness.

And that, perhaps, is Jung's greatest victory. He knew his ideas would be mishandled. He knew his name would be hashtagged, quoted, sold, and diluted. And yet, he also knew that the shadow cannot be silenced forever. Misuse or not, it will find us. It always does.

Chapter 15

The Cultural Shadow – Myths, Movies, & Archetypes

If you want to see the shadow in action, you do not need to lie on a couch or keep a journal. Just turn on the television. Open your phone. Step into a cinema. Watch what the culture adores, who it crucifies, and where it projects its hunger. Jung did not live to see Instagram, Marvel, or mass cancel culture, but he predicted all of them. Why? Because the unconscious never goes out of fashion. It only changes costumes.

Freud, poor Freud, would still be wringing his hands about the libido and our infantile fixations. He would call superheroes wish-fulfilment fantasies, idols for repressed man-children.

Jung would smile and say, "Yes, but do you not see the archetypes screaming through them?" The Hero, the Trickster, the Wise Old Mentor, the Great Mother - our screens are flooded with these eternal forms. They are not mere entertainment. They are mirrors of the collective psyche. The Marvel Cinematic Universe is not just a franchise. It is the pantheon of a generation's mythology, our attempt to digest power, destruction, and redemption in digestible two-hour portions.

And what of the villains? Here the shadow is clearest. We project onto them everything we refuse to admit about ourselves. Thanos carries our repressed lust for control. The Joker embodies chaos we cannot confess. Darth Vader shows us the cost of denying fear until it curdles into domination. These figures terrify us because they are us - magnified, mythologised, stripped of politeness. Jung's words echo: "The shadow is a moral problem that challenges the whole ego-personality." The problem is not that villains exist on screen. The problem is that they exist in us.

But culture does not stop with fiction. Celebrities are crucified for sins the collective will not own. The very traits we bury - greed, lust, vanity, arrogance - are projected onto them until the mob demands sacrifice. When an actor cheats, a singer overdoses, or a politician lies, the outrage is disproportionate because the shadow is at work. The cancel storm is not simply moral indignation. It is projection, pure and unfiltered. Freud would call it hysteria. Jung would call it ritual. Either way, it reveals that the shadow never disappears; it only changes its stage.

This is where my own works circle back, because the shadow is not confined to culture "out there." It bleeds through every layer of our lives. In Activate the Subconscious, I traced how overstimulation numbs us to these deeper archetypal forces - we scroll but we do not see, we consume without recognising that what we consume is consuming us. In Shadow Work Demystified, I exposed how the personal exercises of honesty bleed naturally into the collective sphere: how the irritations we feel at politicians, bosses, or influencers are projections of the selves we refuse to admit. And in Shadow Work Evolution, I confessed what Jung already knew: that cultural evolution is impossible without individuals facing their shadows first. The macro begins in the micro. The collective shadow cannot integrate until we do.

Still, it is tempting to despair. Our myths seem hollow. Our celebrities break. Our politics rot. Freud would shrug: civilisation, after all, is built on repression and always will be. But Jung offers a more scandalous hope: that the shadow's return is not an apocalypse but an invitation. When a culture begins projecting wildly, when its myths falter, when its collective figures collapse under the weight of our disowned traits, it is not the end. It is the chance for integration. The shadow has risen because we are ready, or at least in need.

The emotional trigger here is stark. Look around you. Every public outrage, every viral scandal, every blockbuster you adore, every news story that sickens you - all of it is shadow. And if you dare to admit it, you will see yourself in it. The culture is not separate from you. It is you, multiplied. Your denied desires, your hidden grief, your disowned hunger - all dancing on the stage of the collective. To ignore this is to live in illusion. To embrace it is to live in reality, messy and terrifying as it is.

And so we end where we began. Freud remains embarrassed, a relic of analysis that cannot survive TikTok. Jung stands taller than ever, the Godfather of Shadow Work, laughing softly at the irony that his deepest insights are now performed on screens he never knew existed. The myths change, the archetypes endure, and the shadow waits patiently for us to finally turn and bow.

If you are willing, the theatre is already open. The actors are playing their parts. The only question left is whether you will keep hurling stones from the crowd, or step onto the stage and admit the role you were born to play.

The Offer You Cannot Refuse

Jung never watched *The Godfather*, but he played the part more convincingly than any film could script. The Godfather is not merely a patriarch, not simply a father figure, but the keeper of secrets, the silent witness to the shadow that underpins loyalty and betrayal, honour and violence. He knows every family and every empire is built as much on lies as it is on love. He does not pretend otherwise. He carries it, he consecrates it.

Jung did the same for psychology. Freud wanted the clean authority of the founding father. He wanted neat theories, disciples who obeyed, a fortress of analysis that kept darkness under clinical lock and key. Jung broke away, not to reject psychology, but to baptise it. He opened the cellar Freud kept bolted and declared the shadow sacred. That act - heretical, dangerous, necessary - is why I call him the Godfather of Shadow Work. He refused to collude with illusion.

In The Godfather, *Michael Corleone's* tragedy is not that he has a shadow, but that he refuses to face it. He becomes it blindly, allowing it to devour everything he once swore to protect. Jung's invitation is the opposite. He does not demand obedience, he demands confrontation. He sits at the table, lights dimmed, and places his offer before you: look into the shadow or be ruled by it. Integrate, or perish by fragments.

That is the offer you cannot refuse. Not because it is gentle, but because it is real. You can turn away, but the shadow will not. You can delay, but it will wait. You can deny, but it will seep through every dream, every projection, every person you despise, every scandal that enrages you, every hunger that unsettles you. Jung knew this. He lived it. And he dared to tell us the truth.

Before I take my own seat in the Author's Chair, before I confess what Jung's torch has illuminated in me, let this stand as the final word on his legacy: Jung's psychology is not safe, not polite, not clean. It is dangerous, necessary, alive. Like The Godfather, it is about masks and betrayals, loyalty and exile, shadow and survival. And like The Godfather, it offers you no escape, only a choice.

Face your shadow, or be ruled by it. That is Jung's offer. And it is one you cannot refuse.

From the Author's Chair

Why I Keep Returning to Jung

I have spent so many years writing about the shadow that sometimes I forget why I started. It wasn't ambition, not really. It wasn't the hunger to be an authority, or to put my name on a shelf beside Jung's. It began in silence. It began with the unease I could not explain, the restless nights, the failures I could not ignore. I did not pick up Jung because I thought he was fashionable. I picked him up because I was drowning.

Freud offered explanations. They were clever, sharp, sometimes seductive. But they were not enough. They made me feel smaller, reduced to a bundle of drives and repression. Jung made me feel larger, not because he flattered me, but because he dared me to carry more than I thought I could. He spoke of archetypes, the shadow, the Self, and something inside me recognised the truth. It was not theory, it was memory. As though I had always known, and he had simply reminded me.

That is why I keep returning to Jung. Because he does not let me escape. Every time I think I've finished with him, another shadow rises. Every time I believe I've mapped the psyche, he hands me a torch and points me into another cavern. He embarrasses me, unsettles me, humbles me. He makes me face the parts of myself I would rather dress up or bury. And yet, in the same breath, he offers a kind of grace: you are not broken for having a shadow. You are human.

When I wrote *Activate the Subconscious*, I thought I was writing about silence and stillness. But really, I was writing about fear - my own, mostly - the fear that if I stopped producing, I would vanish. When I wrote *Shadow Work Demystified*, I thought I was writing a map for others. In truth, I was begging myself for one. And when I wrote *Shadow Work Evolution*, I realised the truth: there is no final map. Only the courage to keep going deeper, even when the cave feels endless.

Now, with this book, with Jung at my shoulder like the Godfather of Shadow Work, I see the thread. It is not about mastery. It is not about answers. It is about honesty. Jung keeps dragging me back to the raw, uncomfortable honesty of living. He refuses my masks. He dismantles my illusions. He hands me my fear and whispers, "Here. This is yours. Now integrate it."

And so I keep returning. Because to leave him would be to leave myself.

Watching Myself from Above

Sometimes I imagine stepping outside of myself, rising above, and watching the life I've lived as though it belonged to someone else. It is a strange vantage point - humbling, humiliating, and oddly liberating. From up there, I do not see an expert or an author. I see a man fumbling, a man often afraid, a man who wears masks without even realising it. I see myself at a desk, scribbling theories as if words could protect me from collapse. I see myself pretending to be competent when I felt anything but.

From above, it looks almost comical - all the effort spent polishing a persona, all the fear poured into maintaining a mask. Yet I also see the cracks. The moments when the shadow broke through, when I snapped at someone I loved, when I sabotaged opportunities out of fear, when I drowned in silence because I was too ashamed to admit how loud my inner world really was. Those cracks, from this higher view, are not mistakes. They are doorways. They are where Jung entered, quietly but insistently, reminding me that the shadow is not my enemy but my unfinished self.

I watch myself returning to his works again and again - Activate the Subconscious, Shadow Work Demystified, Shadow Work Evolution - and I realise each book was less a gift to others and more a breadcrumb trail for me. Each one was me whispering to myself: "Do not stop. Do not run. Go deeper." From the ground, it felt like struggle. From above, it looks like survival.

And then something stranger happens. From this vantage point, I also see light. I see the moments I dared to confront what terrified me, the days I admitted failure without excuse, the nights I let myself cry without shame. These were not grand victories. They were quiet acts of integration. They were the places where the shadow was no longer a monster, but a companion. From above, they gleam like small lanterns in a long corridor.

Jung said that individuation was not perfection but wholeness, and now, watching myself, I see what he meant. My wholeness is not found in shining moments of clarity. It is found in the jagged edges, in the mess, in the places I wished were not mine. And yet, they are mine. They always were.

From above, I see a man still learning, still stumbling, still afraid. But I also see a man refusing to turn away.

And maybe that is enough. Maybe that is all Jung ever asked of us - not that we conquer the shadow, but that we stop running from it.

A Final Word to You

If you have read this far, then you have already taken a risk. You have allowed Jung's voice - and mine - to sit with you, to disturb you, to press against the walls you have built. You have not skimmed lightly. You have stayed. And that staying matters.

But let me be clear. This book is not the end. It is not your certificate, not your graduation, not your tidy closure. It is only an invitation, one more offer you cannot refuse. The shadow you carry is already awake, already restless, already waiting for you to stop pretending. Reading about it is not enough. You must face it.

I cannot walk with you when the lights are off and the memories come back. I cannot sit beside you when jealousy burns, when fear grips your chest, when failure humiliates you. That work belongs to you. But what I can tell you - what Jung told me, again and again - is that you are not broken for feeling these things. You are not weak for carrying darkness. You are not lost for stumbling.

The shadow does not come to destroy you. It comes to complete you.

So leave these pages not with comfort, but with courage. Leave knowing that the most frightening parts of you are also the most alive. Leave knowing that the next time fear arrives, or failure crushes, or darkness whispers, you are being invited to step closer to your own wholeness.

This is the path. This is the cost. This is the gift.

I keep returning to Jung because he refused illusion. He refused to let me believe I could live half a life. He showed me that wholeness is worth every failure, every humiliation, every tear. And now, I leave that same torch in your hands.

Do not put it down.

APPENDIX

Curiosity Corner

The Godfather Quotes and Shadow Lessons

Sometimes wisdom hides in unexpected places. Francis Ford Coppola's The Godfather is not a psychology textbook, but it is a parable of shadow. Each line whispers truths about loyalty, fear, betrayal, and the masks we wear. Read them not as movie dialogue but as mirrors of the psyche. A shadow clad in the suit of cinema.

i. **"I'm gonna make him an offer he can't refuse."** The shadow is not polite. It does not ask for permission. It makes its presence felt whether we like it or not. Jung would say: you cannot refuse the invitation to face you.

ii. **"Keep your friends close, but your enemies closer."** Our greatest enemy often lives within. Keeping it closer is the first step to integration.

iii. **"A man who doesn't spend time with his family can never be a real man."** Behind the literal family, think of the psychic family: the Persona, Shadow, Anima/Animus, and Self. To exile one is to remain unfinished.

iv. **"Revenge is a dish best served cold."** Revenge is projection - anger frozen and redirected outward. Integration asks: what part of me am I trying to punish?

v. **"It's not personal, Sonny. It's strictly business."** The ego loves to rationalise the shadow's eruptions. But shadow eruptions are always personal. They show you what you cannot hide.

vi. **"Great men are not born great, they grow great."**
Wholeness is not given. It is forged through struggle, fear, and failure - exactly as Jung taught.

The Godfather and Jung belong to different worlds, but their shadows overlap. Both remind us that denial is costly, that every mask hides a price, and that the offer of integration is one you cannot refuse.

Jungian Quotes That Still Haunt Us

These are not lines to be skimmed. They are to be lived with, wrestled with, returned to when the night is long. Jung's words are not philosophy on a page, they are arrows aimed at the heart of anyone who dares to look inward.

i. **"Until you make the unconscious conscious, it will direct your life and you will call it fate."** A warning and a prophecy. The shadow ignored is the life unlived, shaping you from the back row.

ii. **"Your visions will become clear only when you can look into your own heart. Who looks outside, dreams; who looks inside, awakes."** The pull of distraction is ancient, but the revolution is inward. The heart is where the truth has always been hiding.

iii. **"I am not what happened to me, I am what I choose to become."** The past is heavy, but Jung will not let you collapse under it. He reminds us the self is not a grave, but a becoming.

iv. **"Knowing your own darkness is the best method for dealing with the darknesses of other people."** Compassion is not found in denial. It is born in the shared recognition of our hidden wounds.

v. **"The privilege of a lifetime is to become who you truly are."** The word "privilege" here is no accident. Wholeness is not granted, it is earned. Few will pay the price.

vi. **"Where love rules, there is no will to power, and where power predominates, there love is lacking."** This is not sentiment but challenge. What are you serving - love, or domination?

vii. **"In all chaos there is a cosmos, in all disorder a secret order."** What terrifies you may yet be guiding you. The task is not to escape chaos, but to see what is hidden inside it.

viii. **"One does not become enlightened by imagining figures of light, but by making the darkness conscious."** Jung's most brutal truth. Enlightenment is not about chasing light, but turning to face the dark.

References & Further Reading

The works of Carl Jung provide the foundation:

1. Memories, Dreams, Reflections
2. The Archetypes and the Collective Unconscious
3. Modern Man in Search of a Soul
4. Psychology and Alchemy
5. The Red Book

For those seeking entry points into shadow work and Jungian thought, contemporary resources include:

6. Murray Stein – Jung's Map of the Soul
7. James Hollis – Why Good People Do Bad Things
8. Robert A. Johnson – Owning Your Own Shadow

And then, the reflections from additional books that shaped this manuscript most directly:

9. Activate the Subconscious – Jason A. Solomon, B.Ed.
10. Shadow Work Demystified – Jason A. Solomon, B.Ed.
11. Shadow Work Evolution – Jason A. Solomon, B.Ed.

Each of these speaks not as abstract theory but as lived testimony, pathways into the practical, emotional, and sometimes painful process of confronting what Jung first named.

Companion Reading

This book, Jung, the Godfather of Shadow Work, is one voice in a larger conversation - what I have called Shadow Work Psychology. If you want to continue the journey, these books stand beside it as companions:

Shadow Work Demystified:

A clear doorway into the foundations of working with the shadow, accessible yet uncompromising.

Shadow Work Evolution:

A deeper exploration of the messy, non-linear process of integration, grounded in lived experience.

Activate the Subconscious:

A guide to stillness, silence, and the practices that open space for shadow work to unfold.

Together, they form a series, each one different, each one incomplete without the others. Read them not as manuals, but as mirrors. Let them provoke, unsettle, and guide you into your own work.

Glossary Jungian Terms

i. **Active Imagination** – A technique developed by Jung to dialogue with unconscious images and figures, often through visualisation, writing, or art.

ii. **Anima / Animus** – Archetypal inner figures representing the contrasexual aspect of the psyche: the feminine side of a man (anima) and the masculine side of a woman (animus).

iii. **Archetypes** – Universal patterns or symbols arising from the collective unconscious, shaping behaviour, dreams, myths, and culture. Examples include the Mother, the Hero, the Trickster.

iv. **Collective Unconscious** – The deepest layer of the psyche, shared across humanity, containing archetypes and inherited memory traces.

v. **Complex** – A cluster of emotionally charged ideas and memories centred on a theme, often rooted in personal trauma or repression.

vi. **Ego** – The centre of consciousness, organising thoughts, identity, and daily functioning, but only a small part of the whole psyche.

vii. **Individuation** – The lifelong process of integrating unconscious contents into consciousness, leading toward wholeness of self.

viii. **Persona** – The mask we wear to meet society's expectations, often hiding aspects of our true nature.

ix. **Projection** – The unconscious transfer of one's own unwanted traits or emotions onto another person.

x. **Self** – The totality of the psyche, conscious and unconscious, and the organising principle of individuation.

xi. **Shadow** – The repressed, denied, or hidden parts of the psyche, often containing both destructive tendencies and neglected strengths.

xii. **Synchronicity** – Jung's idea of meaningful coincidences, where inner and outer events align in ways that defy pure chance.

xiii. **Transference** – The redirection of feelings for one person onto another, often seen in therapeutic relationships.

In Closing

You have travelled with me through Jung's world of shadow and light. You have read of archetypes, masks, fear, failure, and the slow, unfinished work of becoming whole. But the shadow does not live in these pages, it lives in you.

Books can open a door, yet they cannot walk you through. That next step belongs to you. Reflection, practice, and the willingness to keep looking into the places you would rather turn away from - this is where shadow work begins to take root. For that reason, I built a Shadow Work AI Companion: https://shadow-work.ai

A living companion designed to walk with you beyond these chapters. It is not therapy, not a substitute for human connection, but it is a space to keep the conversation alive, to keep Jung's questions echoing in your own life, and to remind you that the work never ends.

If your shadow is the whisper in the dark, this companion is the candle you carry forward. It will not hand you answers, it will invite you to ask braver questions. Do not leave this book unchanged. Let this be a beginning, not an ending.

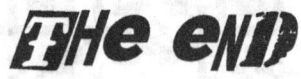

www.ingramcontent.com/pod-product-compliance
Lightning Source LLC
Chambersburg PA
CBHW070558160426
43199CB00014B/2540